SO-AIV-572

Inside the NFL

Pittsburgh Steelers

BY ZACH WYNER

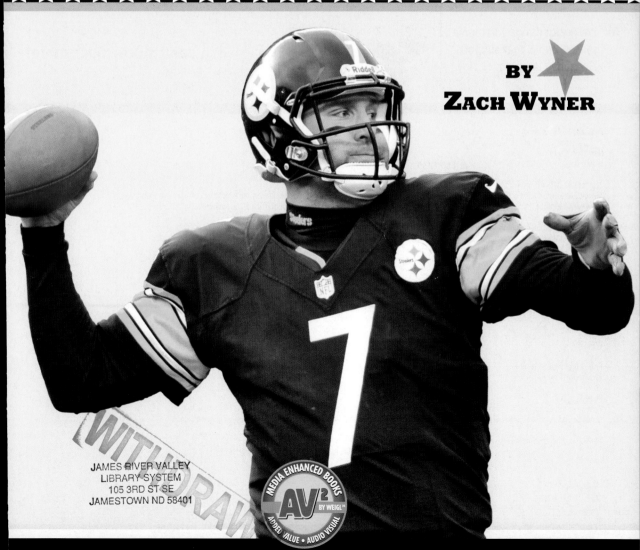

JAMES RIVER VALLEY
LIBRARY SYSTEM
105 3RD ST SE
JAMESTOWN ND 58401

WITHDRAWN

MEDIA ENHANCED BOOKS
AV2 BY WEIGL™
ADDED VALUE • AUDIO VISUAL

AV² provides enriched content that supplements and complements this book. Weigl's AV² books strive to create inspired learning and engage young minds in a total learning experience.

Your AV² Media Enhanced books come alive with...

Audio
Listen to sections of the book read aloud.

Key Words
Study vocabulary, and complete a matching word activity.

Go to **www.av2books.com,** and enter this book's unique code.

Video
Watch informative video clips.

Quizzes
Test your knowledge.

BOOK CODE

H957912

Embedded Weblinks
Gain additional information for research.

Slide Show
View images and captions, and prepare a presentation.

AV² by Weigl brings you media enhanced books that support active learning.

Try This!
Complete activities and hands-on experiments.

... and much, much more!

Published by AV² by Weigl
350 5th Avenue, 59th Floor
New York, NY 10118
Websites: www.av2books.com   www.weigl.com

Copyright © 2015 AV² by Weigl
All rights reserved. No part of this publication may be reproduced, stored in a retrieval system, or transmitted in any form or by any means, electronic, mechanical, photocopying, recording, or otherwise, without the prior written permission of the publisher.

Library of Congress Cataloging-in-Publication Data available upon request.
Fax our Publishing Records department for details: 1-866-449-3445

ISBN 978-1-4896-0878-9 (hardcover)
ISBN 978-1-4896-0880-2 (single-user eBook)
ISBN 978-1-4896-0881-9 (multi-user eBook)

Printed in the United States of America in North Mankato, Minnesota
1 2 3 4 5 6 7 8 9 0 18 17 16 15 14

042014
WEP150314

Project Coordinator Aaron Carr
Art Director Terry Paulhus

Photo Credits
Every reasonable effort has been made to trace ownership and to obtain permission to reprint copyright material. The publishers would be pleased to have any errors or omissions brought to their attention so that they may be corrected in subsequent printings.

Weigl acknowledges Getty Images as its primary image supplier for this title.

Pittsburgh Steelers

CONTENTS

Introduction

For many years, the Pittsburgh Steelers, the American Football Conference's (AFC) oldest team, shifted from bad, to mediocre, to bad again. Founded in 1933 as the Pittsburgh Pirates, they didn't make their first playoff appearance until 1947, a game that they lost, 21-0. After that game, things did not improve. In fact, between 1933 and 1971, the Steelers were one of the lowest-achieving franchises in all of professional sports, with a 0-2 win-loss **postseason** record over a period of 39 years.

Then something remarkable happened. A franchise known for its futility underwent a complete change. A series of brilliant draft picks propelled the Steelers to four **Super Bowl** titles in six years, and the disappointments of the past were suddenly dwarfed by the triumphs of the present.

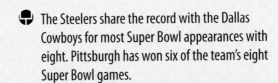

The Steelers share the record with the Dallas Cowboys for most Super Bowl appearances with eight. Pittsburgh has won six of the team's eight Super Bowl games.

A National Football League (NFL) **dynasty** blossomed in Pittsburgh. The Steelers changed from a laughingstock into one of the greatest franchises in NFL history, and Steeler Nation was born.

Ben Roethlisberger has been the starting quarterback for the Steelers since 2004.

Steelers

Stadium Heinz Field

Division American Football Conference (AFC) North

Head coach Mike Tomlin

Location Pittsburgh, Pennsylvania

NFL Championships 1974, 1975, 1978, 1979, 2005, 2008

Nicknames Steel Curtain, Blitzburgh

27
Playoff Appearances

6
Super Bowl Championships

20
Division Titles

History

VICTORY

Pittsburgh has played in, and won more, AFC Championship Games than any other team in the conference. The Steelers are 8-7 in their 15 AFC title games.

In 1978, Terry Bradshaw became the first quarterback to win three Super Bowls. The next year, he became the first to win four.

After just two winning seasons in their first 39 years, the Steeler transformation began in 1969 with the hiring of coach Chuck Noll, and the drafting of "Mean Joe" Greene. The following year, the Steelers moved into Three Rivers Stadium and drafted quarterback, and future **Pro Bowler,** Terry Bradshaw. Within a few years, the Steelers grew from 1-13 cellar dwellers to Central Division champions. In the 1972 **playoffs**, the Steelers beat the Oakland Raiders on a ridiculous catch, called the "Immaculate Reception," by rookie running back Franco Harris.

With an offense led by **hall of famers** Terry Bradshaw, Franco Harris, Lynn Swann, Mike Webster, and John Stallworth, and a "Steel Curtain" defense comprised of Pro Football Hall of Famers Jack Lambert, Jack Ham, Joe Greene, and Mel Blount, the Pittsburgh Steelers dominated the 1970s. They won four Super Bowl titles and the loyalty of many fans.

The hiring of coach Bill Cowher, along with a new crop of defensive stars like Rod Woodson and Greg Lloyd, brought the Steelers back to prominence in the 1990s. Then, in 2005, Cowher and second-year quarterback Ben Roethlisberger brought Pittsburgh its fifth Super Bowl title. Three years later, head coach Mike Tomlin helped them do it again, as the Steelers became the first NFL team to win six Super Bowls.

Though he retired in 2004, Rod Woodson still holds the NFL record with 12 interception returns for touchdowns.

The Stadium

Heinz Field can hold 65,050 cheering fans.

Located along the banks of the Ohio River, on the North side of Pittsburgh is Heinz Field. Replacing historic Three Rivers Stadium, home to the Steelers during their run of four Super Bowl titles in six years, has not been easy. However, the designers of Heinz Field were intent upon creating a structure that provided a link to the past.

Heinz Field has sold out for every single Steelers home game since the team opened play there in 2001.

Among the material used to construct Heinz Field is 12,000 tons of steel, an alloy famously produced in Pittsburgh. Another important feature of the stadium is the Great Hall, which contains a collection of Steelers memorabilia. Highlighting these items are the lockers of former Steeler greats "Mean Joe" Greene and Franco Harris. The Hall also contains memorabilia from the University of Pittsburgh, as the University of Pittsburgh Panthers are co-occupants of the stadium.

When Heinz Field first opened in 2001, its 27-foot by 96-foot (8-meter by 30-meter) Sony Jumbotron was the largest scoreboard in the NFL. This scoreboard has since been replaced by two LED Daktronics video displays of roughly the same size.

Hungry Steelers fans head to Grid Iron Grill for foot-long hot dogs, kielbasa, hot smoked sausage, and bratwurst.

Where They Play

CANADA

Washington — 30
Oregon
Montana
North Dakota
Minnesota
Lake Superior
Idaho
South Dakota
Wisconsin — 23
29
Wyoming
22
15
Nevada
Utah
Nebraska
Iowa
24
14
13
Illinois
California
Colorado
Kansas
Missouri
UNITED STATES
31
16
Arizona
New Mexico
Oklahoma
Arkansas
32
17
Texas
Missis
Louisiana
Pacific Ocean
12
27
Alaska
Hawai'i
MEXICO
Gulf of Mexico

0 500 Miles
0 500 km

0 100 Miles
0 100 km

AMERICAN FOOTBALL CONFERENCE

EAST	NORTH	SOUTH	WEST
1 Gillette Stadium	5 FirstEnergy Stadium	9 EverBank Field	13 Arrowhead Stadium
2 MetLife Stadium	★ 6 Heinz Field	10 LP Field	14 Sports Authority Field at Mile High
3 Ralph Wilson Stadium	7 M&T Bank Stadium	11 Lucas Oil Stadium	15 O.co Coliseum
4 Sun Life Stadium	8 Paul Brown Stadium	12 NRG Stadium	16 Qualcomm Stadium

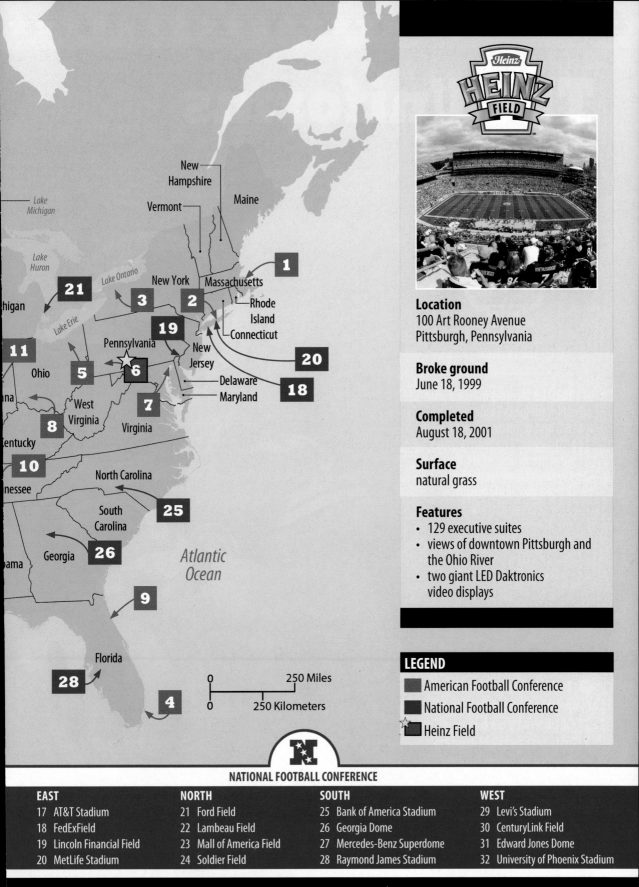

Location
100 Art Rooney Avenue
Pittsburgh, Pennsylvania

Broke ground
June 18, 1999

Completed
August 18, 2001

Surface
natural grass

Features
- 129 executive suites
- views of downtown Pittsburgh and the Ohio River
- two giant LED Daktronics video displays

LEGEND
- American Football Conference
- National Football Conference
- ☆ Heinz Field

250 Miles
250 Kilometers

NATIONAL FOOTBALL CONFERENCE

EAST	NORTH	SOUTH	WEST
17 AT&T Stadium	21 Ford Field	25 Bank of America Stadium	29 Levi's Stadium
18 FedExField	22 Lambeau Field	26 Georgia Dome	30 CenturyLink Field
19 Lincoln Financial Field	23 Mall of America Field	27 Mercedes-Benz Superdome	31 Edward Jones Dome
20 MetLife Stadium	24 Soldier Field	28 Raymond James Stadium	32 University of Phoenix Stadium

The Uniforms

In 1943, the Steelers merged with the Philadelphia Eagles for one season, and together they formed the "Steagles." The team's colors were green and white that year, as they wore the Eagles' uniforms.

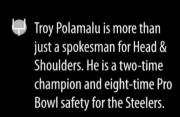 Troy Polamalu is more than just a spokesman for Head & Shoulders. He is a two-time champion and eight-time Pro Bowl safety for the Steelers.

O riginally named the Pittsburgh Pirates, the team changed their name to the Steelers in 1940. Their first uniforms were gold with black stripes. The felt stripes were not just chosen for their looks, as they allowed the ball carrier to hold the ball more securely against his jersey. In 2013, the Steelers' **alternate jersey** was a throwback to this original design.

These days, the Steelers wear essentially the same home and away uniforms that they have worn since 1968. The home jersey is black with white numbers and gold stripes on the sleeves, while the away jersey is white with black numbers and gold stripes on the sleeves. Both jerseys are paired with gold pants.

The Steelers' alternate uniforms were first used during the team's 75th anniversary season in 2007. The uniforms have hung around since, because of their popularity with the fan base.

The Helmets

What's Your Number?

The Steelers and the New York Giants are the only two NFL teams to have the players' numbers on both the front and back of the helmets.

NFL helmet designs have changed over time to improve player safety. Modern helmets are made from lightweight plastic shells that can withstand a great deal of impact.

The Steelers introduced the famous "asteroid" **logo** in 1962. It was based on the "Steelmark" logo used by the American Iron and Steel Institute. The logo consists of three diamond shapes colored yellow, blue, and red. These colors were selected to represent the three materials used to make steel, coal, ore, and steel scrap.

At first, the Steelers had mixed feelings about wearing the American Iron and Steel Institute logo, so before the 1962 season began, they decided to place it only on one side of the helmet. The Steelers' surprising nine-win campaign, combined with the helmet's unique look, brought it the kind of attention that no one anticipated. Before playing in the 1962 Playoff Bowl, the Steelers changed their helmets from gold to black in order to make the logo stand out. The look was instantly appealing, and that appeal never wore off. To this day, it remains unchanged.

In addition to helmets, leg and shoulder pads are required to keep players safe.

The Coaches

23 Chuck Noll is one of only four men to be the head coach of the same franchise for at least 23 years.

Mike Tomlin's coaching career began in 1995 at the Virginia Military Institute. Twelve years and six coaching stops later, he was named the head coach of the Pittsburgh Steelers.

The city of Pittsburgh is what is known as a blue-collar town. It is home to the steel industry that employs many of its citizens, and those citizens share some common traits. They work hard, they complain little, and they expect the same of their football team. It is with this in mind that the Steelers have historically sought out coaches who share the attributes of its residents.

CHUCK NOLL

Chuck Noll knew what it took to excel in professional football. The designer of the "Steel Curtain" defense and the only coach in NFL history to win four Super Bowls, Noll was a great judge of talent. Four of Noll's first five selections in the 1974 **NFL Draft** went on to become hall of famers.

BILL COWHER

Bill Cowher always had to work hard to get a roster spot. The uncertainty he faced during his playing career helped give him the work ethic that made him a successful coach. In 15 seasons in Pittsburgh, Cowher led the Steelers to 10 playoff appearances, two AFC Championships, and one Super Bowl title.

MIKE TOMLIN

Mike Tomlin was the first Pittsburgh coach to win back-to-back division titles in his first two seasons. While the first resulted in a playoff loss, the second ended in a Super Bowl title. Tomlin was the second African American to coach a team to a Super Bowl victory. At the age of 36, he was also the youngest.

The Mascot

Steely McBeam was introduced to the world in 2007 as part of the team's 75th anniversary celebration.

The Steelers mascot is a tall, strong, square-jawed construction worker. His name is Steely McBeam, and many fans across Steeler Nation have noted his striking resemblance to former tough-guy Steeler head coach Bill Cowher.

Steely McBeam was conceived in 2007, the brainchild of die-hard Steelers fan Diane Roles of Butler County, Pennsylvania. According to Diane, the "Mc" in "McBeam" was intended to pay tribute to the Irish roots the Rooney family, long-time owners of the Steelers. The "Beam" was included because of Pittsburgh's famous production of steel beams.

Famous for waving their Terrible Towels, the fans in Pittsburgh also have a mascot known as the Terrible Fan.

The second most popular name submitted to Pittsburgh's Name-That-Mascot contest was "Footbally McPittsburgh."

Legends of the Past

Many great players have suited up in the Steelers black and gold. A few of them have become icons of the team and the city it represents.

Hines Ward

In the Steelers' record books, Hines Ward sits atop a long list of great wide receivers that includes hall of famers Lynn Swan and John Stallworth. In addition to holding the team record for most receptions (1,000), receiving yards (12,083), and most receiving touchdowns (85), Ward is also regarded as one of the finest blockers to ever play the wide receiver position. Born in Seoul, South Korea, but raised in Georgia, Ward is the second foreign-born player to be named Super Bowl MVP. In Super Bowl XL, his five receptions for 123 yards and a touchdown were crucial in leading the Steelers to victory.

Position Wide Receiver
Seasons 14 (1988–2001)
Born March 8, 1978, in Seoul, South Korea

Terry Bradshaw

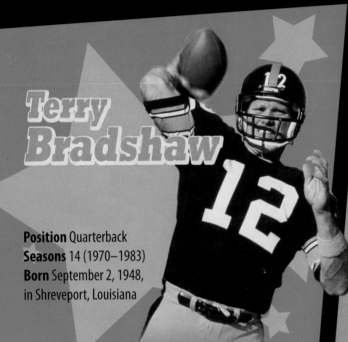

Position Quarterback
Seasons 14 (1970–1983)
Born September 2, 1948, in Shreveport, Louisiana

As a high school student, Terry Bradshaw was a star quarterback who also excelled at track and field, setting a national record for the javelin throw (245 feet, 75 meters). After a stellar career at Louisiana Tech University, the Steelers chose Bradshaw with the number one overall selection in the 1970 NFL Draft. Bradshaw became the first quarterback to win four Super Bowls. In 1978, his finest season as a pro, he led the NFL with 28 touchdown passes, and was named league **most valuable player (MVP)**. In the Steelers' thrilling 35-31 Super Bowl win over the Dallas Cowboys, Bradshaw threw for 318 yards and four touchdowns.

Rod Woodson

In 10 seasons with the Pittsburgh Steelers, Rod Woodson made seven Pro Bowls and was named a first-team **All-Pro** six times. Opposing teams not only had to worry about Woodson covering their best wide receiver, they had to worry about his ability to turn a punt return or an interception into a touchdown. In his career, Woodson returned two punts, two kickoffs, and 12 interceptions for touchdowns. Woodson's finest season may have come in 1993, when he had eight interceptions, two forced fumbles, two **sacks**, 95 tackles, and was named NFL Defensive Player of the Year.

Position Cornerback/Kick Returner/Punt Returner
Seasons 17 (1987–2003)
Born March 10, 1965, in Fort Wayne, Indiana

Jerome Bettis

Known affectionately as "The Bus" because of his 5-foot, 11-inch, 250-pound frame, Jerome Bettis could move those 250 pounds as fast or faster than any man that size in NFL history. "The Bus" rushed for more than 1,000 yards in each of his first six seasons in Pittsburgh, making three Pro Bowls in the process. His 10,571 yards and 78 rushing touchdowns are second only to Steeler legend Franco Harris. In Bettis' last game in Pittsburgh, he scored three touchdowns to help the Steelers earn a playoff spot. A month later, in Bettis' final professional game, the Steelers won their fifth Super Bowl.

Position Running Back
Seasons 13 (1993–2005)
Born February 16, 1972, in Detroit, Michigan

Stars of Today

Today's Steelers team is made up of many young, talented players who have proven that they are among the best players in the league.

Troy Polamalu

A three-sport star (football, baseball, and basketball) in high school, Troy Polamalu's reputation as one of the top football players in the country solidified during his time at the University of Southern California. As a Steeler, Polamalu has exceeded all expectations. An eight-time Pro Bowler and five-time first-team All-Pro, he has been the **centerpiece** of two Super Bowl-winning defenses. In 2010, he jumped from stardom to superstardom, making numerous game-saving plays while recording seven interceptions, 64 tackles, 11 defended passes, a forced fumble, and winning the NFL's Defensive Player of the Year Award.

Position Safety
Seasons 11 (2003–2013)
Born April 19, 1981, in Garden Grove, California

Ben Roethlisberger

S tanding 6 feet, 5 inches, and weighing 240 pounds, "Big Ben" Roethlisberger does not appear fleet of foot. However, his ability to elude the rush and extend plays makes him one of the most feared quarterbacks in the league. Roethlisberger became the youngest starting quarterback to win an NFL Championship when, at the age of 23, he led the Steelers to victory in Super Bowl XL. The two-time Pro Bowler and franchise leader in career **passer rating** did it again in Super Bowl XLIII. In the game's final minutes, Roethlisberger engineered an 88-yard drive that ended with a six-yard touchdown pass and a 27-23 Steelers victory.

Position Quarterback
Seasons 10 (2004–2013)
Born March 2, 1982, in Lima, Ohio

LeVeon Bell

■ n Week 4 of the 2013 NFL season, the Pittsburgh Steelers traveled to London, England, to play the Minnesota Vikings. Rookie Le'Veon Bell returned from an ankle injury suffered in the preseason and showed football fans from across the globe that he had arrived. In his first NFL game, Bell ran for 57 yards and scored two touchdowns. As the season progressed, Bell looked more and more comfortable rushing and receiving. In Week 16, he topped Franco Harris' Steeler record for rushing yards in a single game by a rookie. In a 38-31 win over the Green Bay Packers, Bell gained 124 yards on 26 carries.

Position Running Back
Seasons 1 (2013)
Born February 18, 1992, in Reynoldsburg, Ohio

Antonio Brown

■ n 2011, Antonio Brown's first season as a Steelers wide receiver, he started just three games and still managed to catch 69 passes for 1,108 yards. He also returned kickoffs and punts, bringing his total **all-purpose yards** to 2,211. It was a huge season for the sixth-round draft pick out of Central Michigan University. However, at the time few suspected that within two years, Brown would be breaking Steeler receiving records. In 2013, Brown returned from an ankle injury to become Roethlisberger's primary target. He caught 110 passes and set a Steelers' single-season record with 1,499 receiving yards.

Position Wide Receiver
Seasons 4 (2010–2013)
Born July 10, 1988, in Miami, Florida

All-Time Records

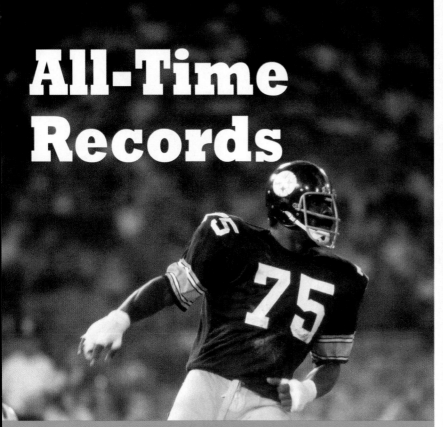

10   Career Pro Bowls

While no one kept track of sacks and tackles in his day, "Mean Joe" Greene tops all Steelers with 10 Pro Bowl appearances.

11,950   Career Rushing Yards

During his time in Pittsburgh, Franco Harris set team records for rushing touchdowns (91) and rushing yards.

JAMES RIVER VALLEY
LIBRARY SYSTEM
105 3RD ST SE
JAMESTOWN ND 58401

12,083 Career Receiving Yards

While he may have a reputation as one of the NFL's best blocking receivers, Hines Ward caught a few passes too, setting franchise records for receptions (1,000) and receiving yards.

34,105
Career Passing Yards

In just 10 seasons, Ben Roethlisberger has surpassed Terry Bradshaw to become the Steelers' all-time passing leader.

57 Career Interceptions

Steelers Hall of Fame cornerback Mel Blount led the league with 11 interceptions in 1974, and holds Pittsburgh's all-time record for career interceptions.

Timeline

Throughout the team's history, the Pittsburgh Steelers have had many memorable events that have become defining moments for the team and its fans.

1940
Tired of the name "Pirates," Art Rooney holds a contest to rename the team. "Steelers," a named that pays tribute to Pittsburgh's largest industry, is selected from a list of entries that includes names such as Condors, Pioneers, Bridgers, Buckaroos, Vulcans, Tubers, and Puddlers.

1970
The **American Football League (AFL)** and NFL merge and the Steelers join the newly formed American AFC. In the 1970 NFL Draft, the Steelers select Terry Bradshaw with the first overall pick, and at the beginning to the season, they move into Three Rivers Stadium.

On January 12, 1975, the Steelers win their first championship, 16-6.

| 1930 | 1940 | 1950 | 1960 | 1970 | 1980 |

1943
With so many young men going off to fight in World War II, the 1943 Steelers do not have enough players to field a team. During the season, they combine with the Philadelphia Eagles and are commonly referred to as the "Steagles."

May 19, 1933
The NFL grants Pittsburgh native Art Rooney's request to start a professional franchise and the Pittsburgh Professional Football Club, Inc. joins the NFL. They go by the name "Pirates," the same name as the Major League Baseball franchise located in Pittsburgh.

1974
Pittsburgh's 1974 draft picks Mike Webster, Lynn Swann, John Stallworth, and Defensive Rookie of the Year Jack Lambert propel the Steelers to a division title. "Mean Joe" Greene is named the NFL's Defensive Player of the Year, and the Steelers win the AFC Championship Game in Oakland to advance to their first Super Bowl.

February 2009

The five-time Super Bowl-champion Steelers face off against the Arizona Cardinals, a team that had not played in an NFL Championship since 1948. After surrendering an early lead, Ben Roethlisberger leads a late 88-yard touchdown drive that gives the Steelers a 27-23 victory and an NFL-record sixth Super Bowl title.

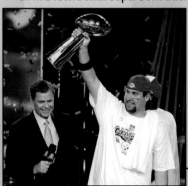

In 2004, Ben Roethlisberger wins Rookie of the Year, and 36-year-old Jerome "The Bus" Bettis makes his sixth and final Pro Bowl.

The Future

After a horrendous 2-6 start to the 2013 season, the Steelers rebound to win six of their final eight games. Roethlisberger threw for more than 4,000 yards for the third time in his career, and Troy Polamalu and Antonio Brown both returned from injury to make the Pro Bowl. In 2014, the Steelers will look to surround their stars with a bit more depth, as they attempt to climb back to the top of the AFC North.

| 1990 | 1995 | 2000 | 2005 | 2010 | 2015 |

In Super Bowl XL, the Steelers beat the Seattle Seahawks, 21-10, becoming the first number six seed to win a Super Bowl.

1992

First-year head coach/ Pittsburgh native Bill Cowher wins Coach of the Year and the Steelers win the AFC Central for the first time since 1984. Barry Foster's 2,034 **yards from scrimmage** earn him Offensive Player of the Year honors, while All-Pro cornerback Rod Woodson records six sacks, four interceptions, four forced fumbles, and 100 tackles.

2010

Rashard Mendenhall, Mike Wallace, and Defensive Player of the Year Troy Polamalu lead the Steelers to 12 wins and the team's eighth conference championship. In Super Bowl XLV against Green Bay, the Steelers cannot quite overcome a 21-3 deficit, and lose a nail biter, 31-25.

Write a Biography

Life Story

A person's life story can be the subject of a book. This kind of book is called a biography. Biographies often describe the lives of people who have achieved great success. These people may be alive today, or they may have lived many years ago. Reading a biography can help you learn more about a great person.

Get the Facts

Use this book, and research in the library and on the Internet, to find out more about your favorite Steeler. Learn as much about this player as you can. What position does he play? What are his statistics in important categories? Has he set any records? Also, be sure to write down key events in the person's life. What was his childhood like? What has he accomplished off the field? Is there anything else that makes this person special or unusual?

Use the Concept Web

A concept web is a useful research tool. Read the questions in the concept web on the following page. Answer the questions in your notebook. Your answers will help you write a biography.

Concept Web

Adulthood
- Where does this individual currently reside?
- Does he or she have a family?

Your Opinion
- What did you learn from the books you read in your research?
- Would you suggest these books to others?
- Was anything missing from these books?

Childhood
- Where and when was this person born?
- Describe his or her parents, siblings, and friends.
- Did this person grow up in unusual circumstances?

Accomplishments off the Field
- What is this person's life's work?
- Has he or she received awards or recognition for accomplishments?
- How have this person's accomplishments served others?

Write a Biography

Help and Obstacles
- Did this individual have a positive attitude?
- Did he or she receive help from others?
- Did this person have a mentor?
- Did this person face any hardships?
- If so, how were the hardships overcome?

Accomplishments on the Field
- What records does this person hold?
- What key games and plays have defined his or her career?
- What are his or her stats in categories important to his or her position?

Work and Preparation
- What was this person's education?
- What was his or her work experience?
- How does this person work; what is the process he or she uses?

Trivia Time

Take this quiz to test your knowledge of the Pittsburgh Steelers.
The answers are printed upside-down under each question.

1 Which famed Steelers coach led Pittsburgh to four Super Bowl titles?

A. Chuck Noll

2 Which Steelers coach is mascot Steely McBeam said to resemble?

A. Bill Cowher

3 How many conference championships have the Steelers won in their history?

A. Eight

4 Which Steeler was the first quarterback to win four Super Bowls?

A. Terry Bradshaw

5 What is the name given to the legions of Steelers fans across the country?

A. Steeler Nation

6 What was the name given to Franco Harris' game-winning catch in the 1972 playoffs?

A. The Immaculate Reception

7 Which Hall of Fame lineman set a team-record with 10 Pro Bowl trips?

A. "Mean Joe" Greene

8 Who is the Steelers' all-time passing leader?

A. Ben Roethlisberger

9 Which Pittsburgh Steeler running back won a Super Bowl in his final professional game?

A. Jerome Bettis

10 What were the Steelers called in 1943, the year they joined forces with the Philadelphia Eagles?

A. Steagles

Key Words

All-Pro: an NFL player judged to be the best in his position for a given season

all-purpose yards: also referred to as combined net yards, all-purpose yards are a statistic that measures total yardage gained on receptions, runs from scrimmage, punt returns, and kickoff returns

alternate jersey: a jersey that sports teams may wear in games instead of their home or away uniforms

American Football League (AFL): a major American Professional Football league that operated from 1960 until 1969, when it merged with the National Football League (NFL)

centerpiece: a player intended to be the focus of attention

dynasty: a team that win a series of championships in a short period of time

hall of famers: a group of persons judged to be outstanding in a particular sport

logo: a symbol that stands for a team or organization

most valuable player (MVP): the player judged to be most valuable to his team's success

NFL Draft: an annual event where the NFL chooses college football players to be new team members

passer rating: a rating given to quarterbacks that tries to measure how well they perform on the field

playoffs: the games played following the end of the regular season; six teams qualify: the four conference winners, and the two best teams that did not finish first in their conference, called the wild cards

postseason: a sporting event that takes place after the end of the regular season

Pro Bowler: NFL players who take part in the annual all-star game that pits the best players in the National Football Conference against the best players in the American Football Conference

sacks: a sack occurs when the quarterback is tackled behind the line of scrimmage before he can throw a forward pass

Super Bowl: the NFL's annual championship game between the winning team from the NFC and the winning team from the AFC

yards from scrimmage: the total of rushing yards and receiving yards from the yard-line on the field from which the play starts

Index

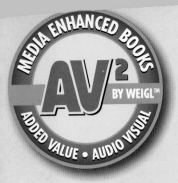

Log on to www.av2books.com

AV² by Weigl brings you media enhanced books that support active learning. Go to www.av2books.com, and enter the special code found on page 2 of this book. You will gain access to enriched and enhanced content that supplements and complements this book. Content includes video, audio, weblinks, quizzes, a slide show, and activities.

AV² Online Navigation

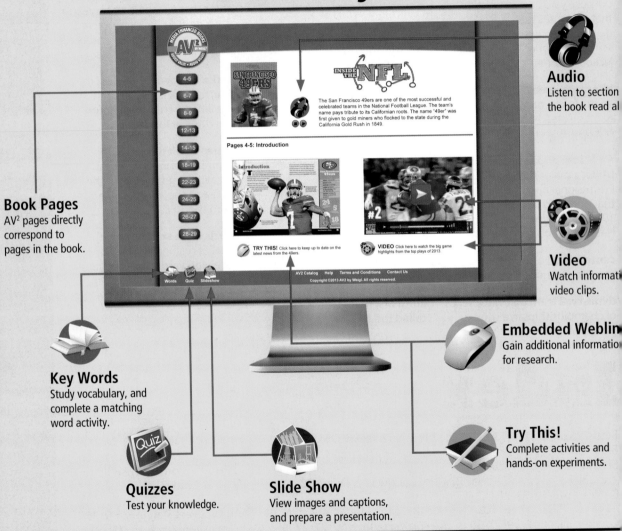

Book Pages
AV² pages directly correspond to pages in the book.

Audio
Listen to section the book read al

Video
Watch informati
video clips.

Embedded Weblin
Gain additional information
for research.

Key Words
Study vocabulary, and complete a matching word activity.

Try This!
Complete activities and hands-on experiments.

Quizzes
Test your knowledge.

Slide Show
View images and captions, and prepare a presentation.

AV² was built to bridge the gap between print and digital. We encourage you to tell us what you like and what you want to see in the future.

Sign up to be an AV² Ambassador at www.av2books.com/ambassador.

Due to the dynamic nature of the Internet, some of the URLs and activities provided as part of AV² by Weigl may have changed or ceased to exist. AV² by Weigl accepts no responsibility for any such changes. All media enhanced books are regularly monitored to update addresses and sites in a timely manner. Contact AV² by Weigl at 1-866-649-3445 or av2books@weigl.com with any questions, comments, or feedback.